This Disney Adventure Belongs to:

I am ____ years old.
This is my ____ visit to Disney.
On this trip, the people with me are:

I am most excited to:

Meet: _____

Ride: _____

Eat: _____

Do: _____

Hear: _____

When you're curious, you find lots of interesting things to do.
-Walt Disney

Match the Quote

"I like Warm Hugs"   "You are a sad, strange little man, and you have my pity."

"Do or do not. There is no try."

"I'm late! I'm late, for a very imporant date!"  "They just can't get my nose right!"

"Never fails! You get in the tub and there's a rub at the lamp."  "Ohana means family. Family means no one gets left behind. Or forgotten."

"I'll get you for this, Pan, if it's the last thing I do!"  "Find something for 'It' to play with, while I think of a plan!"

Alice's Tea Party!

Decorate your teacup, then draw yourself going for a twirl

Mad Hatter Riddles

1. What has a head, a tail is brown and has no legs?

2. I'm light as a feather, yet the strongest man can't hold me for more than 5 minutes. What am I?

3. What comes down but never goes up?

4. In a one-story green house, there was a green person, a green cat, a green computer, a green table, a green shower - everything was green! What color were the stairs?

5. What word becomes shorter when you add two letters to it?

6. What starts with the letter 't', is filled with 't' and ends in 't'?

7. Which weighs more, a pound of feathers or a pound of bricks?

Answers: 1. a penny 2. breath 3. rain 4. No stairs, it was a one-story house 5. short 6. a teapot 7. neither, they both weigh one pound

Design Your Own

TARZAN'S TREEHOUSE

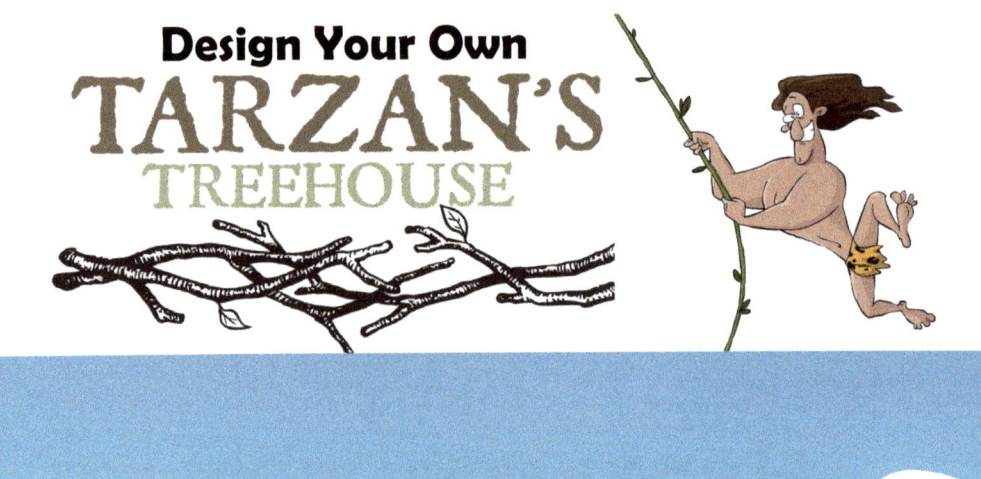

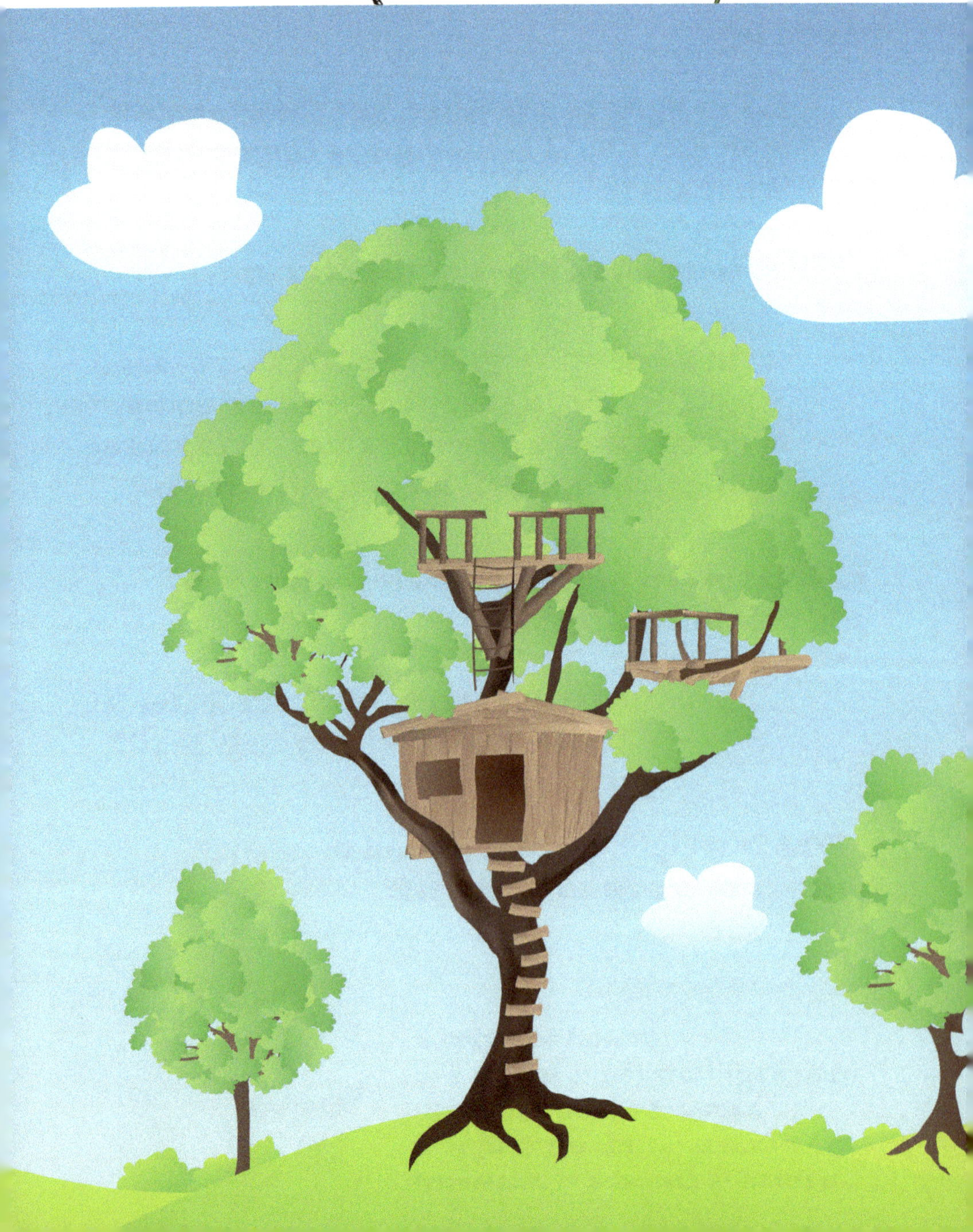

If Tinkerbell gave you enough pixie dust to fly to THREE places, where would you choose and why?

The first place I'd fly is:

Then I would fly to:

Last, I would fly to:

Name These Villains

Help Mickey get to Minnie's House!

Help C-3PO fix R2-D2!

Connect the dots! Start at 1. Be sure to pass over the dark dots for curves.

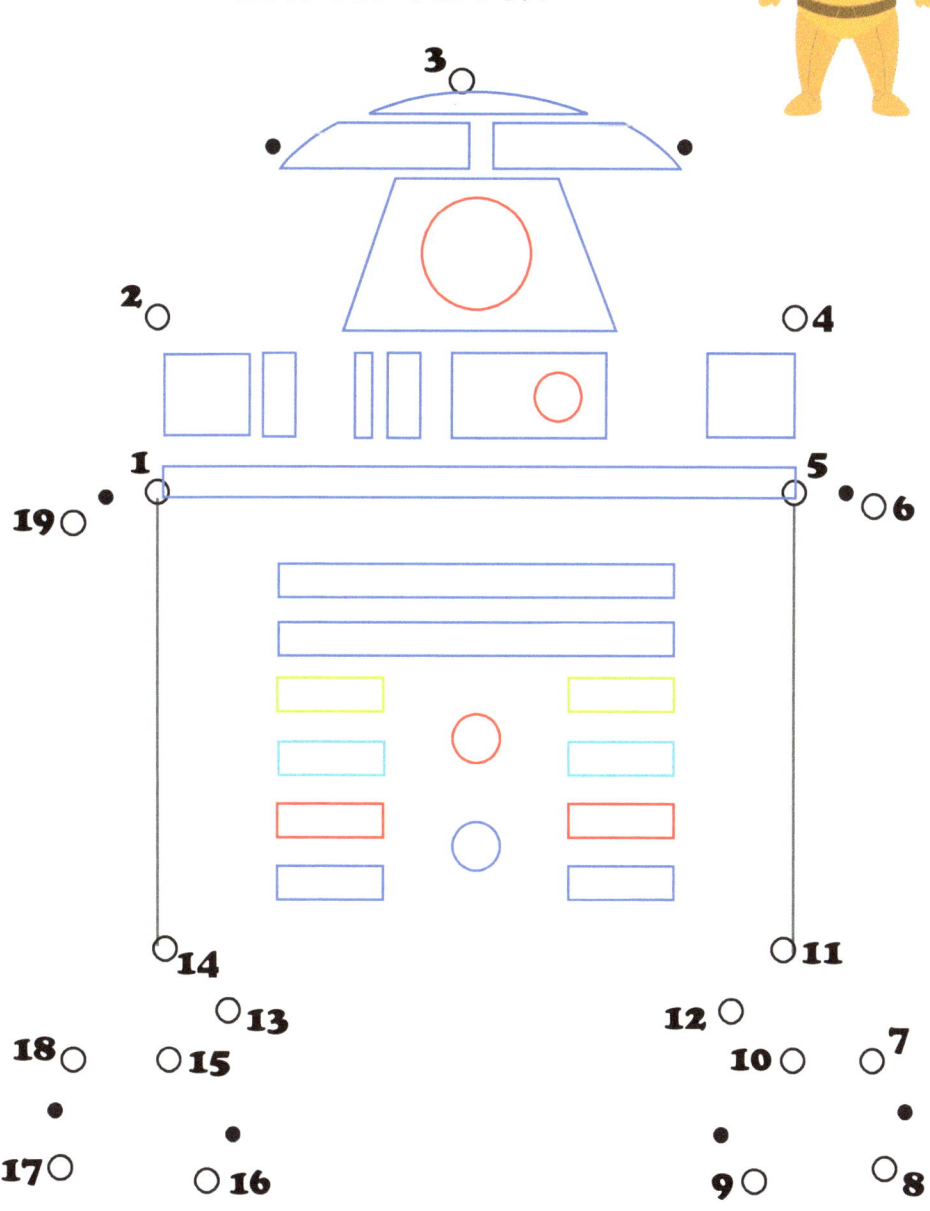

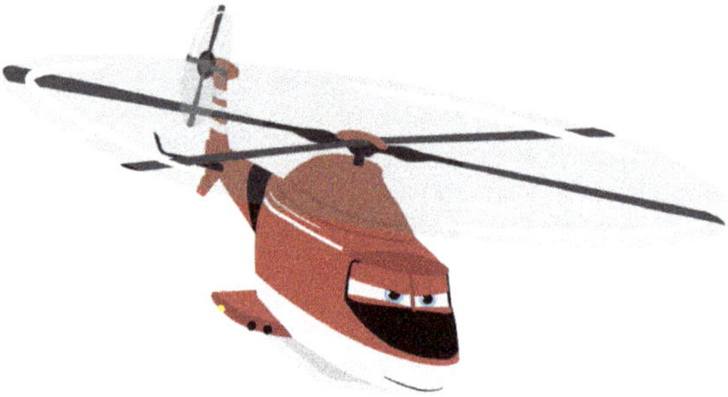

Which Dusty is Different?

1. 
2. 
3.
4.

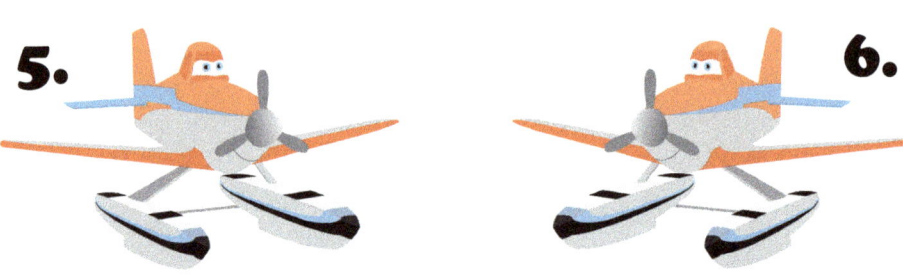

5.
6.

McQueen wants to visit Mater

STAR WARS

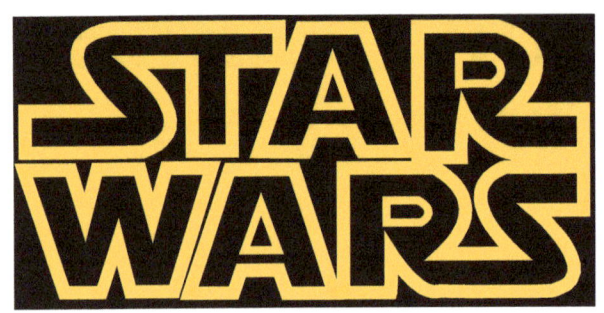

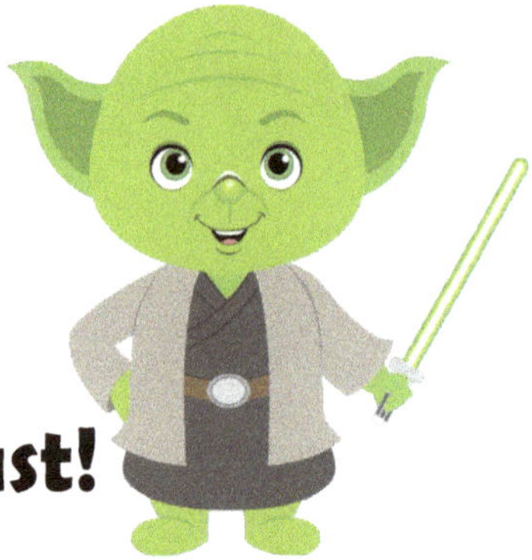

Find the words, you must!

H	A	U	D	E	S	T	R	O	Y	E	R	I
A	V	S	O	S	D	E	W	O	O	K	I	E
M	A	U	L	I	R	P	A	L	D	O	D	T
K	D	T	I	L	O	L	E	I	A	U	A	I
O	E	U	G	O	I	L	O	F	O	R	C	E
A	R	I	H	K	D	E	W	T	O	J	A	F
D	E	A	T	H	S	T	A	R	P	A	S	I
K	A	O	S	A	P	U	W	O	A	B	T	G
L	D	U	A	I	H	W	D	O	I	B	O	H
U	O	A	B	T	A	A	K	P	S	A	I	T
K	S	I	E	P	N	L	O	E	I	T	A	E
E	J	A	R	J	A	R	D	R	A	E	W	R

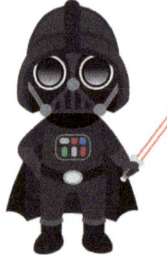

Deathstar
Lightsaber
Han
Leia
Jabba
Trooper

Tiefighter
JarJar
Luke
Destroyer
Wookie

Force
Vader
Droid
Yoda
Maul

Join the Team

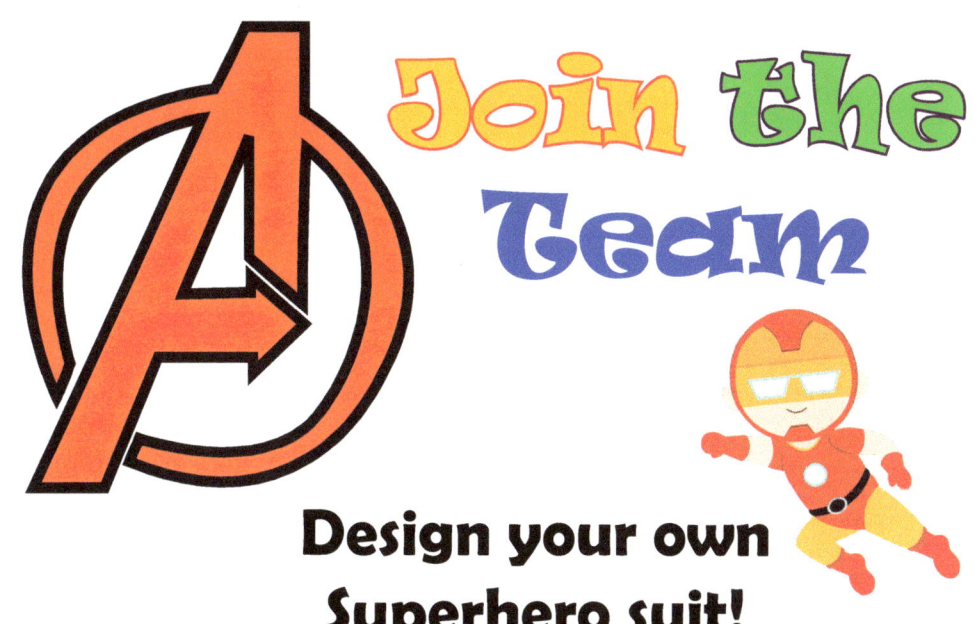

Design your own Superhero suit!

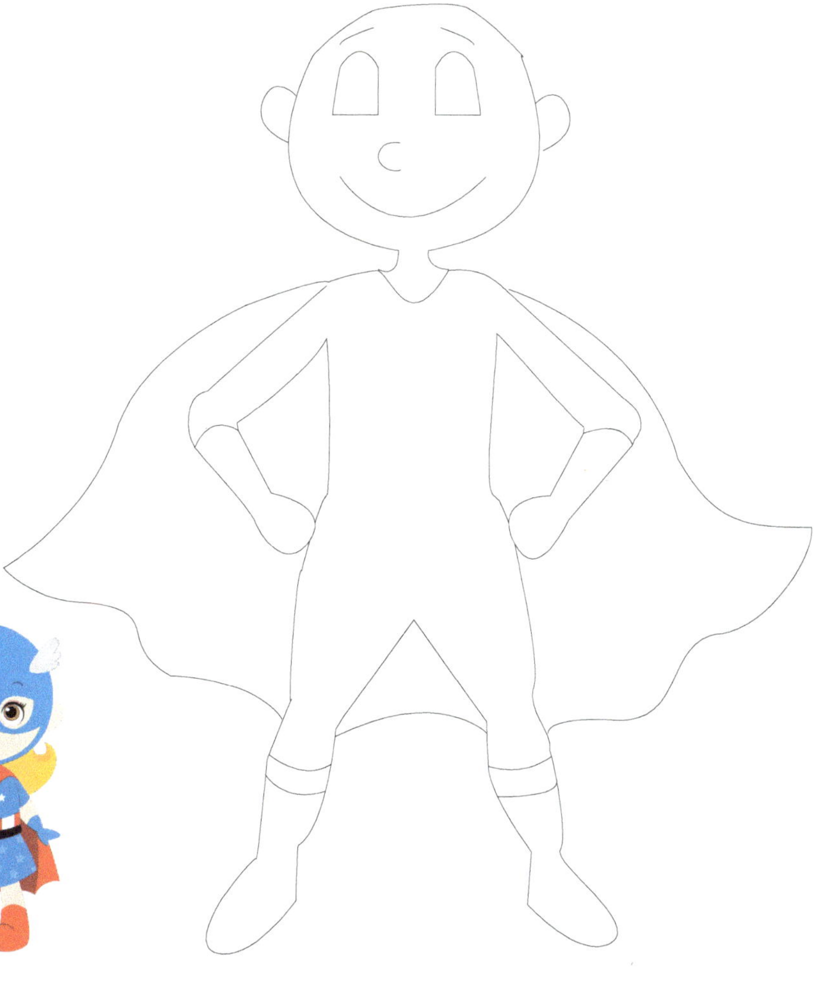

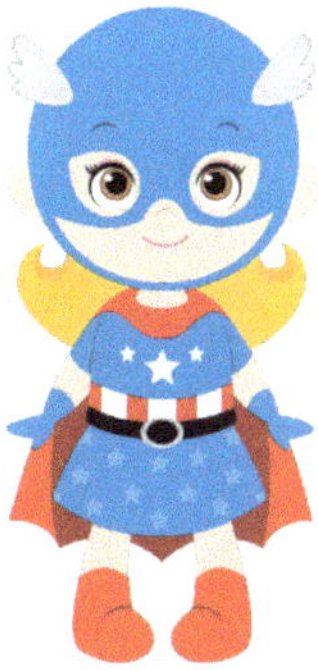

Laugh with Goofy!

Why did the banana go to the hospital?
He wasn't peeling well

What do postal workers do when they're mad?
Stamp their feet

What nails do carpenters hate to hit?
Fingernails

What do you call a king who is only 12 inches tall?
A ruler

How does the ocean say hello?
It waves

Why did the melon jump in the lake?
It wanted to be a watermelon

What did one egg say to the other?
You crack me up

Why can't a bike stand up?
Because it's two tired

Why did the drum take a nap?
It was beat

What room can you NOT go into?
A mushroom

Disney Trivia

Have fun learning some interesting things about favorite Disney movies!

1. The "asante sana squash banana" song that Rafiki sings in The Lion King is an old nursery rhyme in Swahili.

2. Beast's appearance in Beauty and the Beast is an amalgamation of several animals. It's said he has the head of a buffalo, the brow of a gorilla, the body of a bear, the mane of a lion, the tusks of a boar, and the legs and tail of a wolf.

3. The names of the main characters in Frozen sound out the name of the author of the original story the movie is based on. Hans, Kristoff, Anna, Sven = Hans Christian Andersen.

4. It would take about 9.4 million balloons to lift Carl's house in Up.

5. The Disney character WALL-E is named after Walt Disney. (Walter Elias Disney.)

6. Marc Okrand, who created the Klingon and Vulcan languages for Star Trek, create an entire Atlantean language for Atlantis: The Lost Empire.

Match the Characters with their friends!

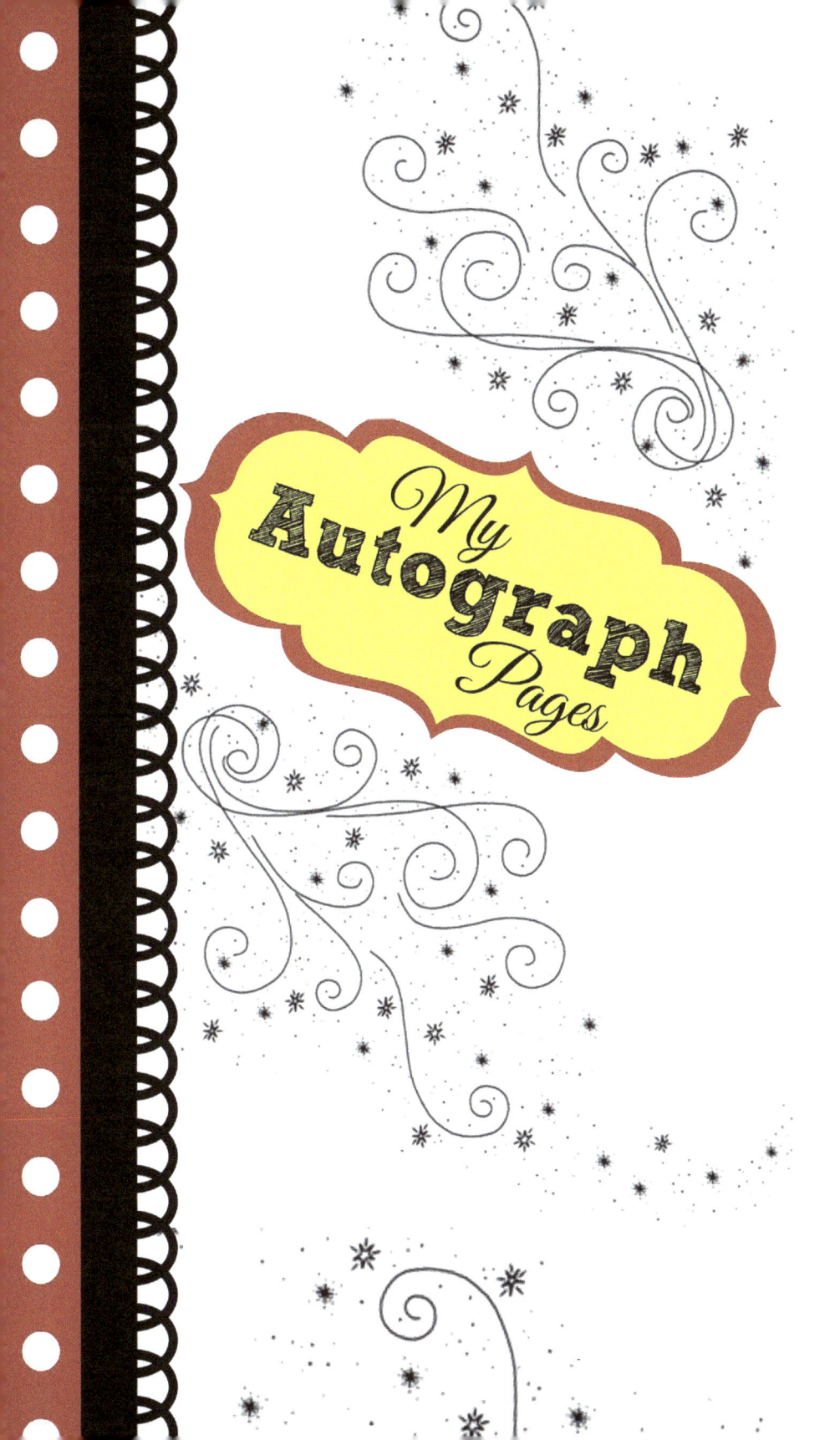

#1 Duck!

Princess Power

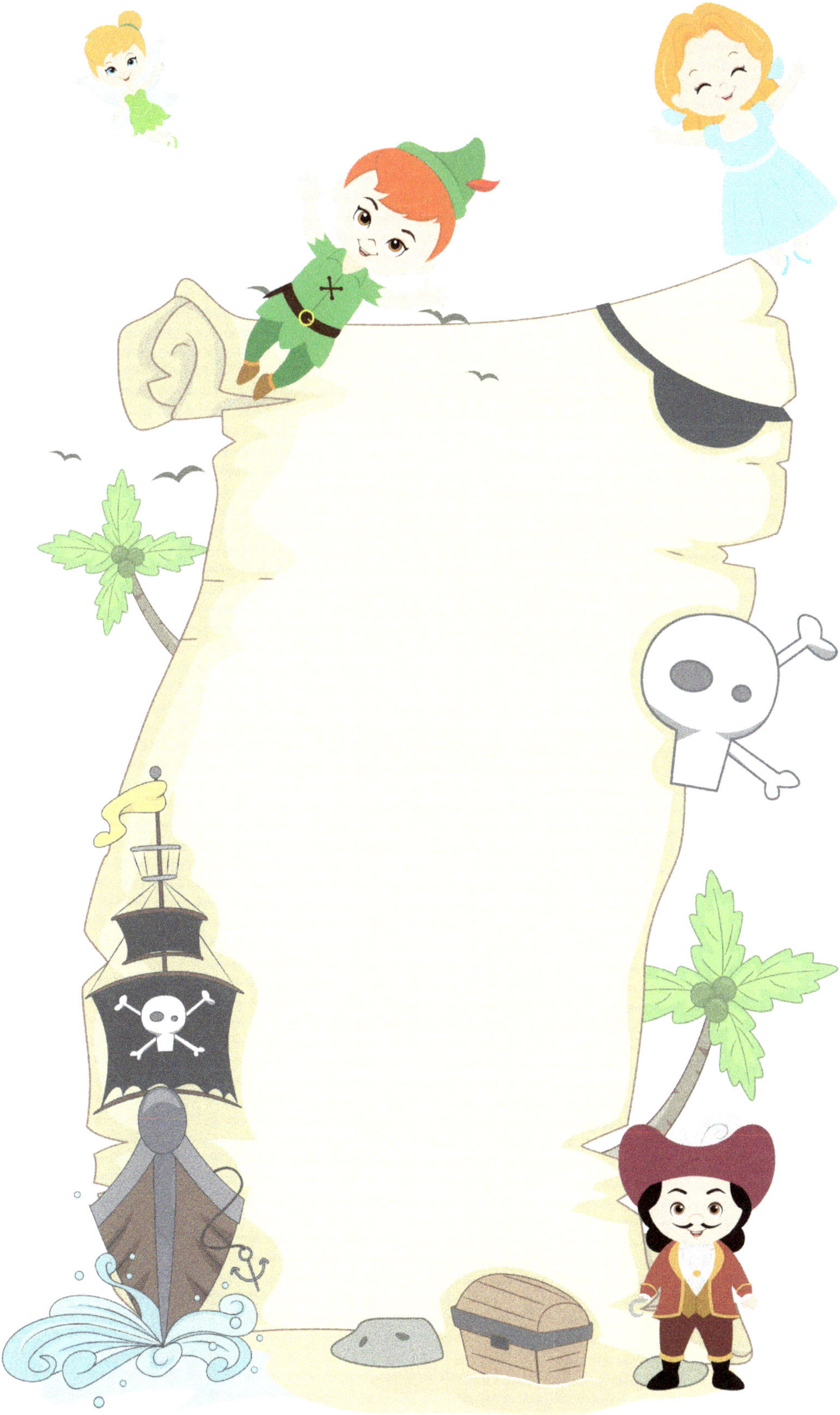

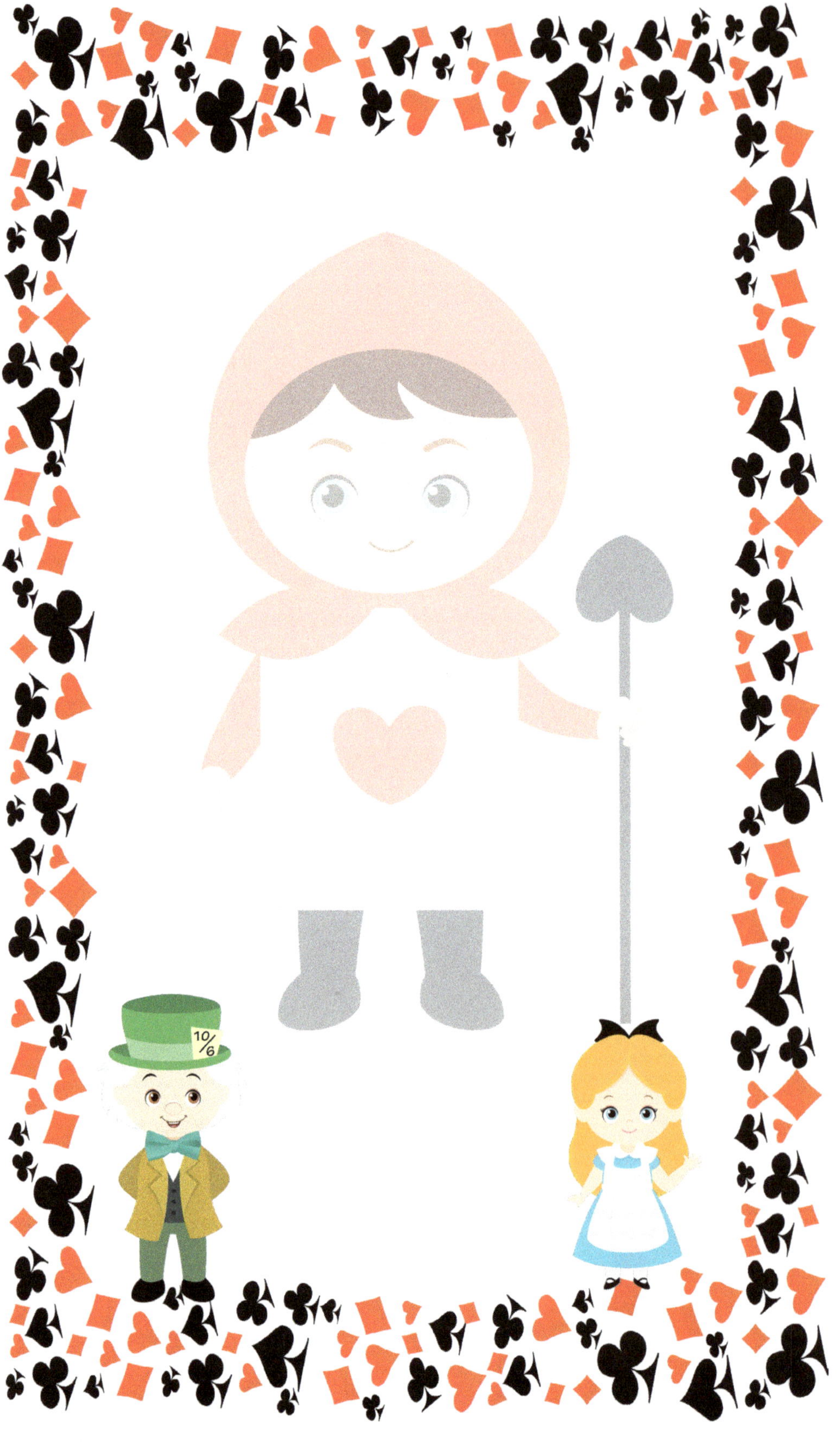
10/6

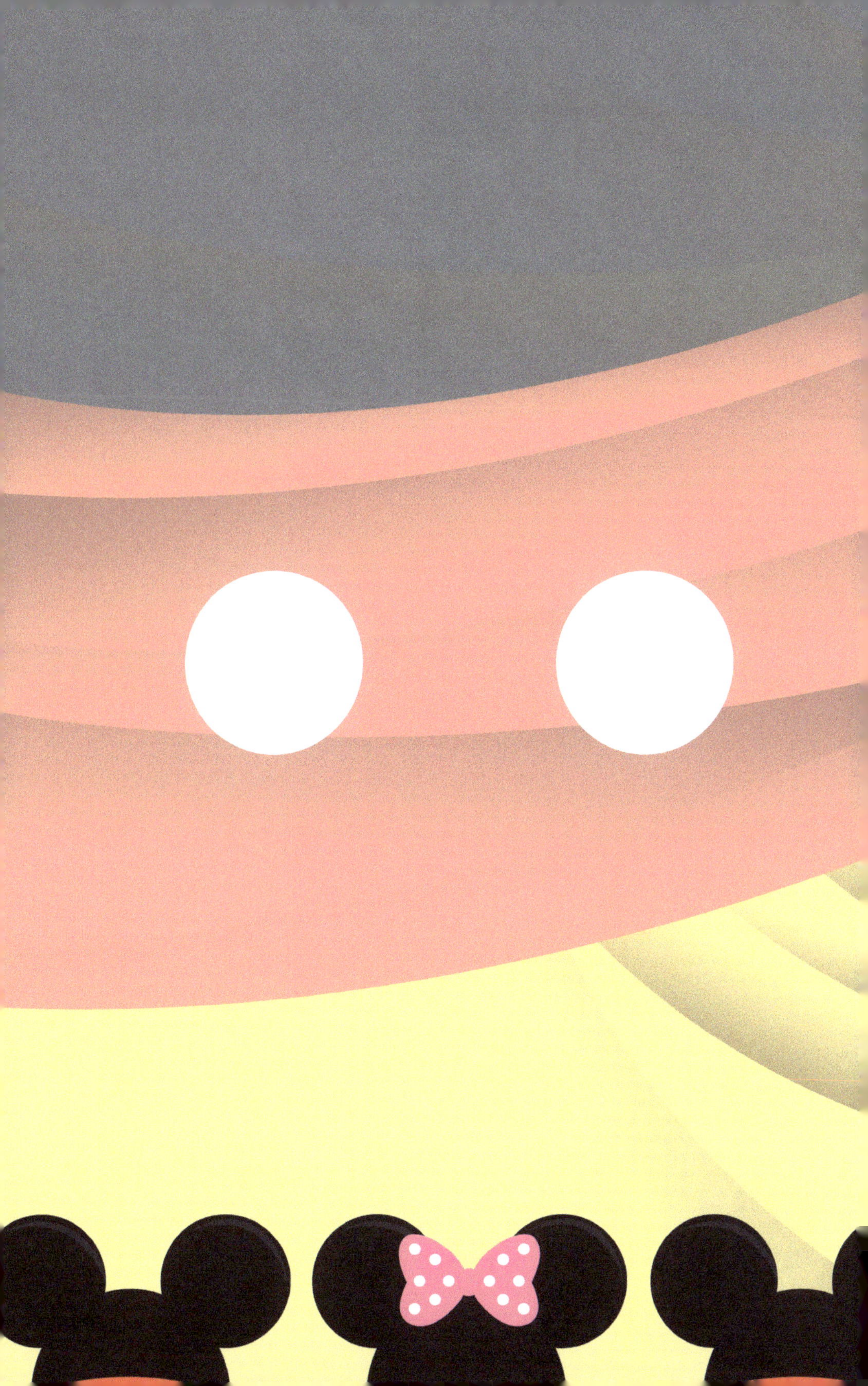

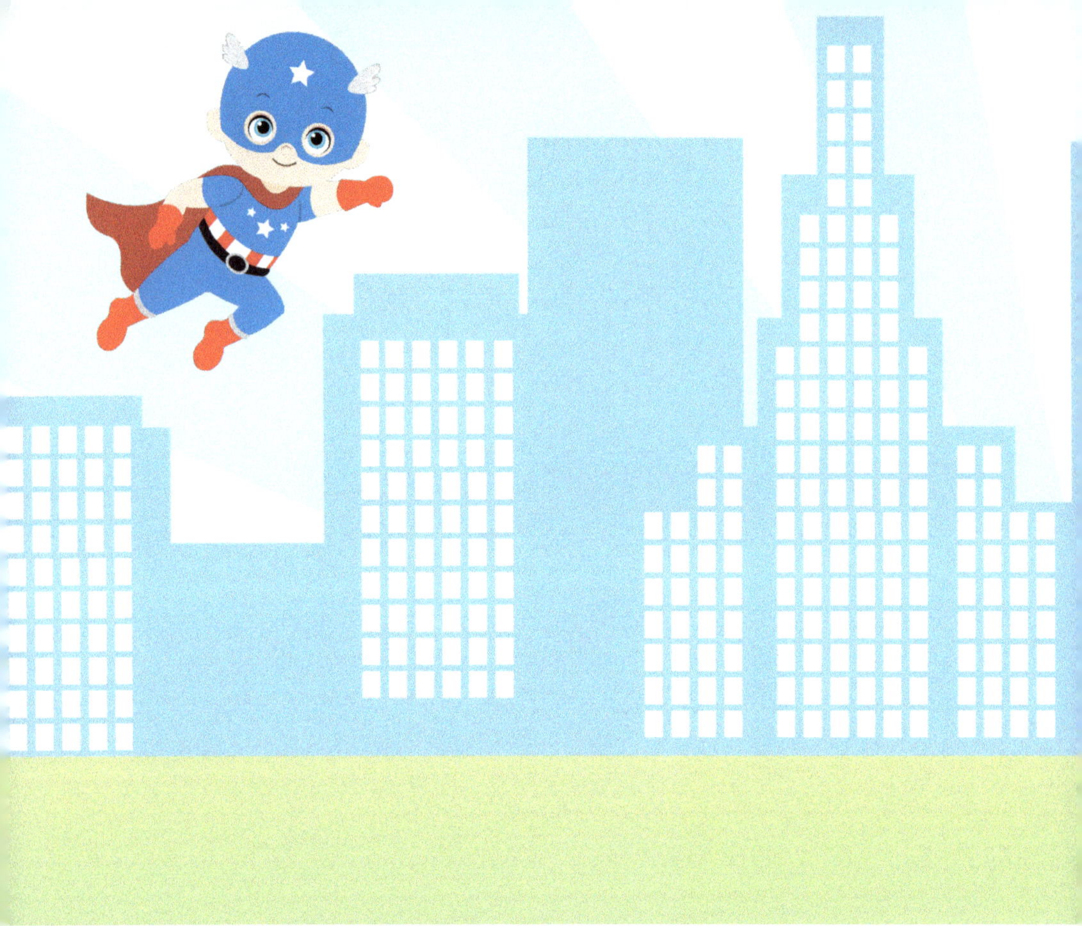

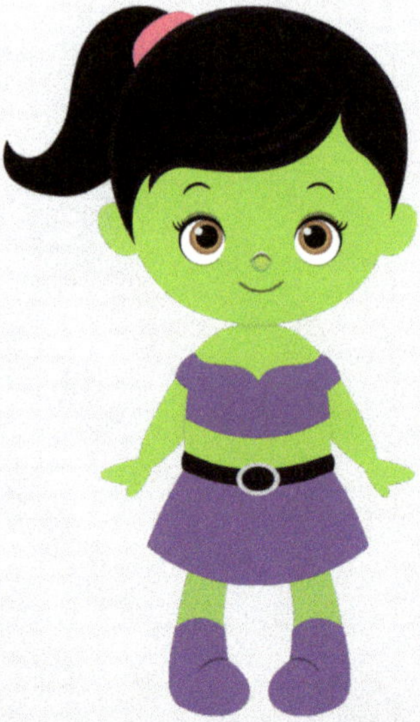

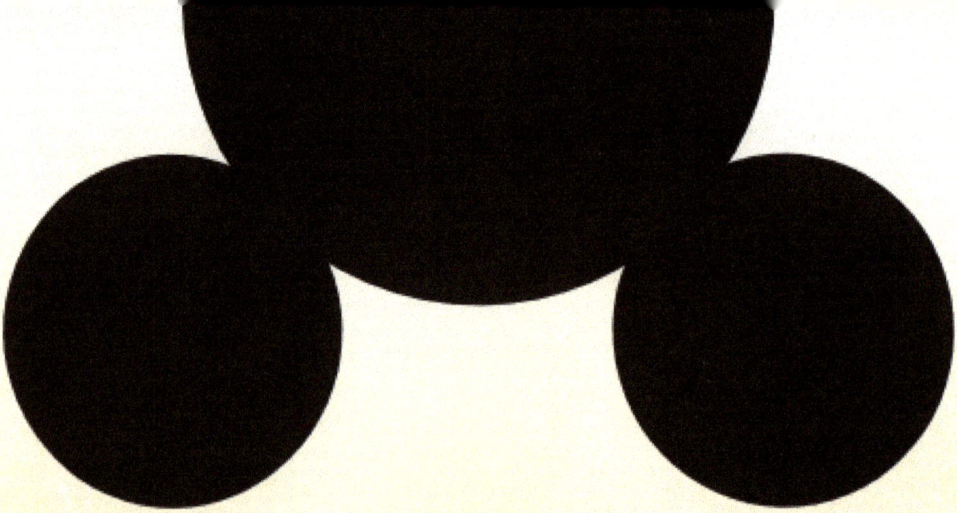

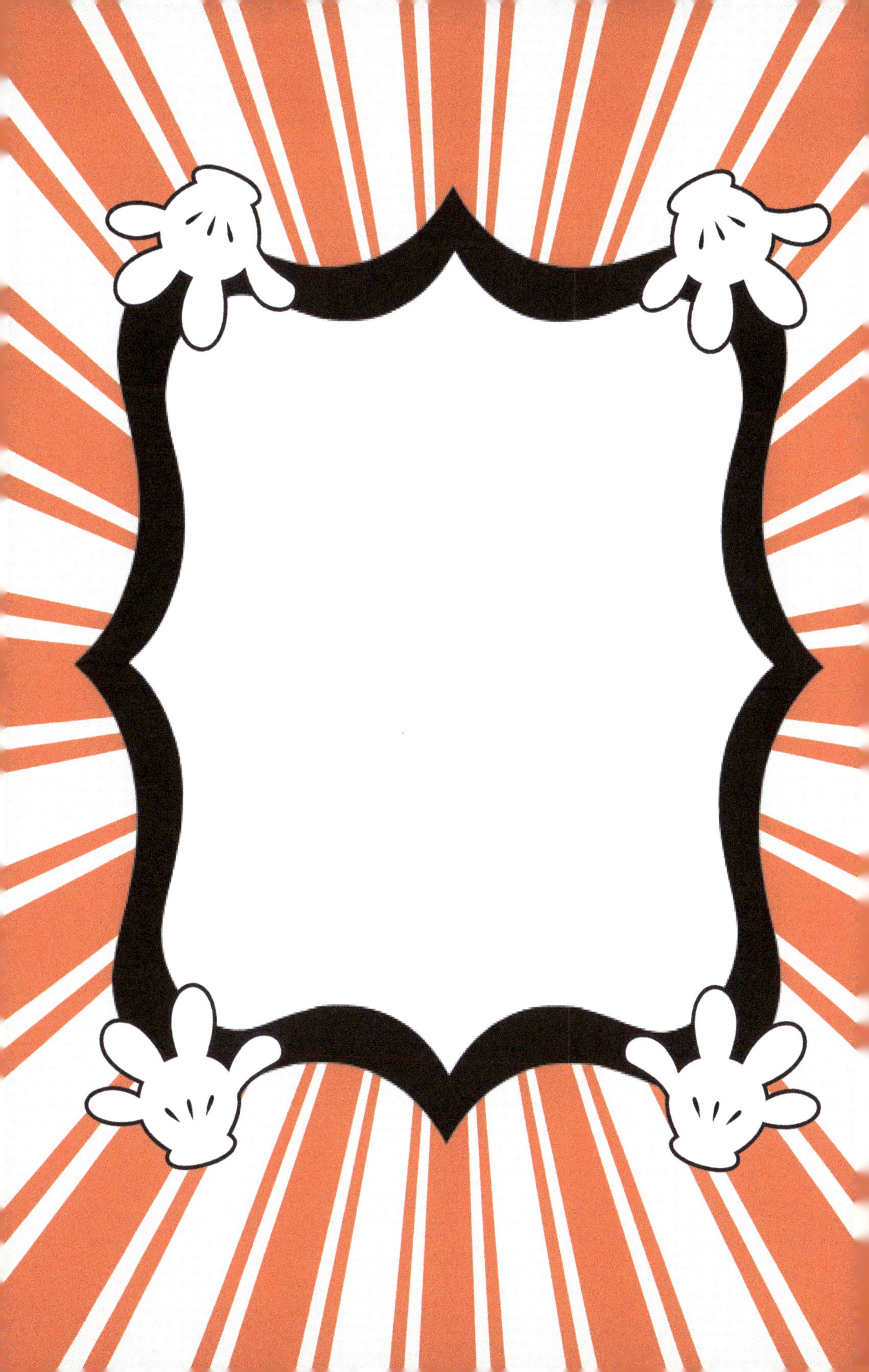

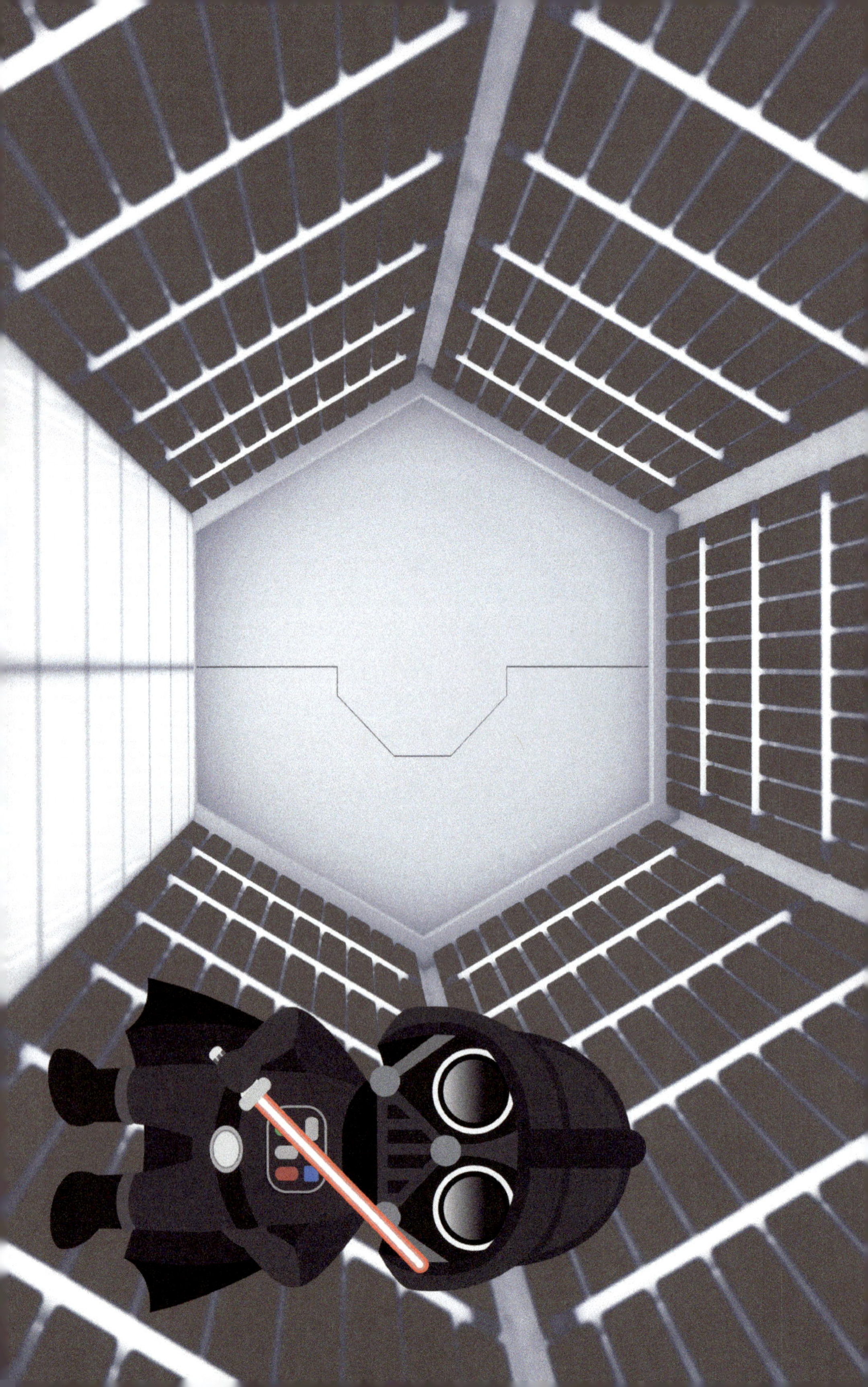

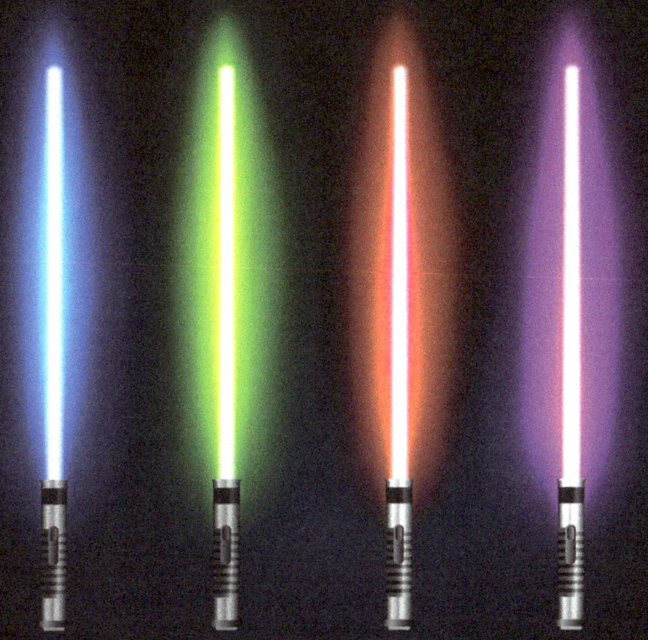

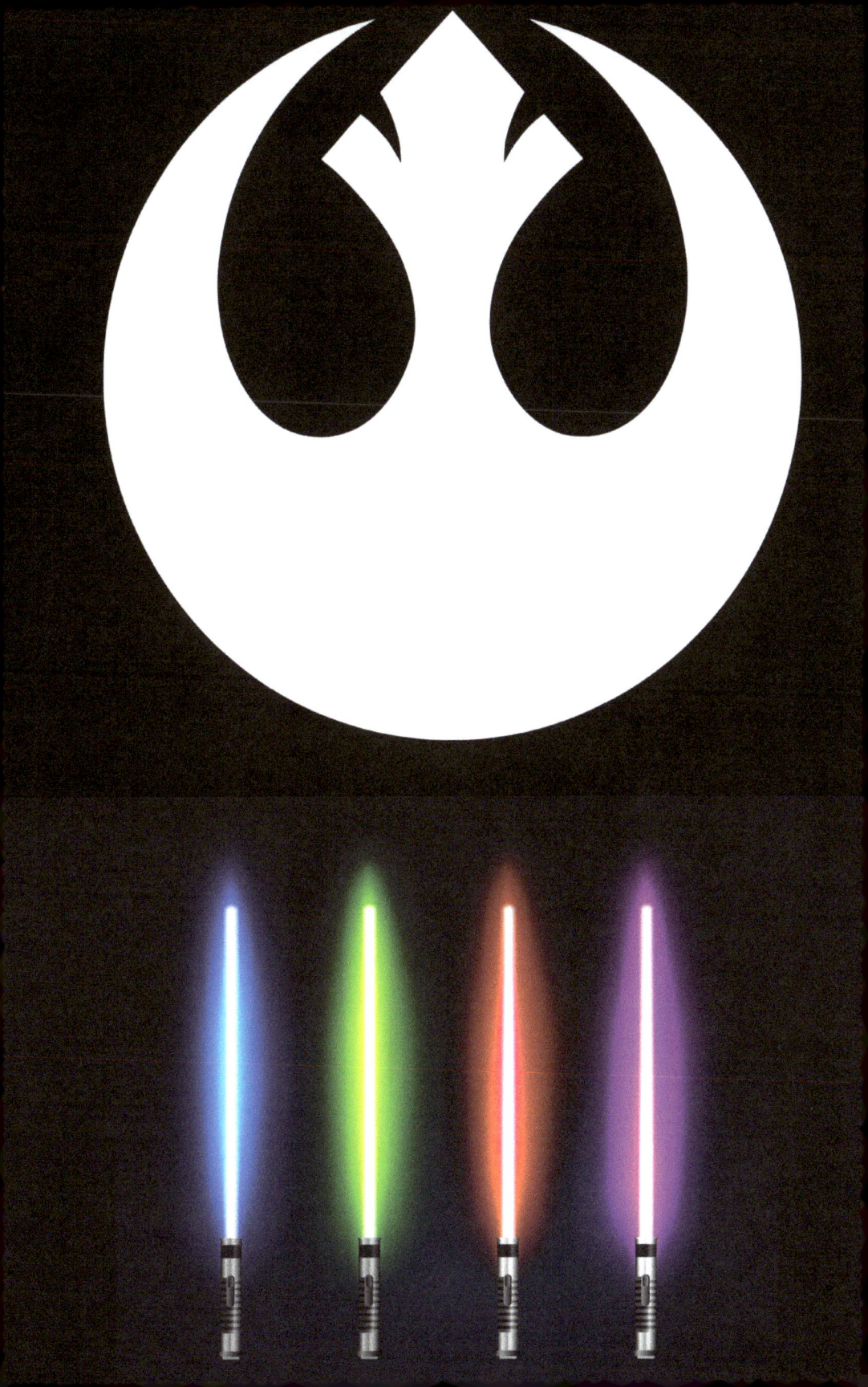

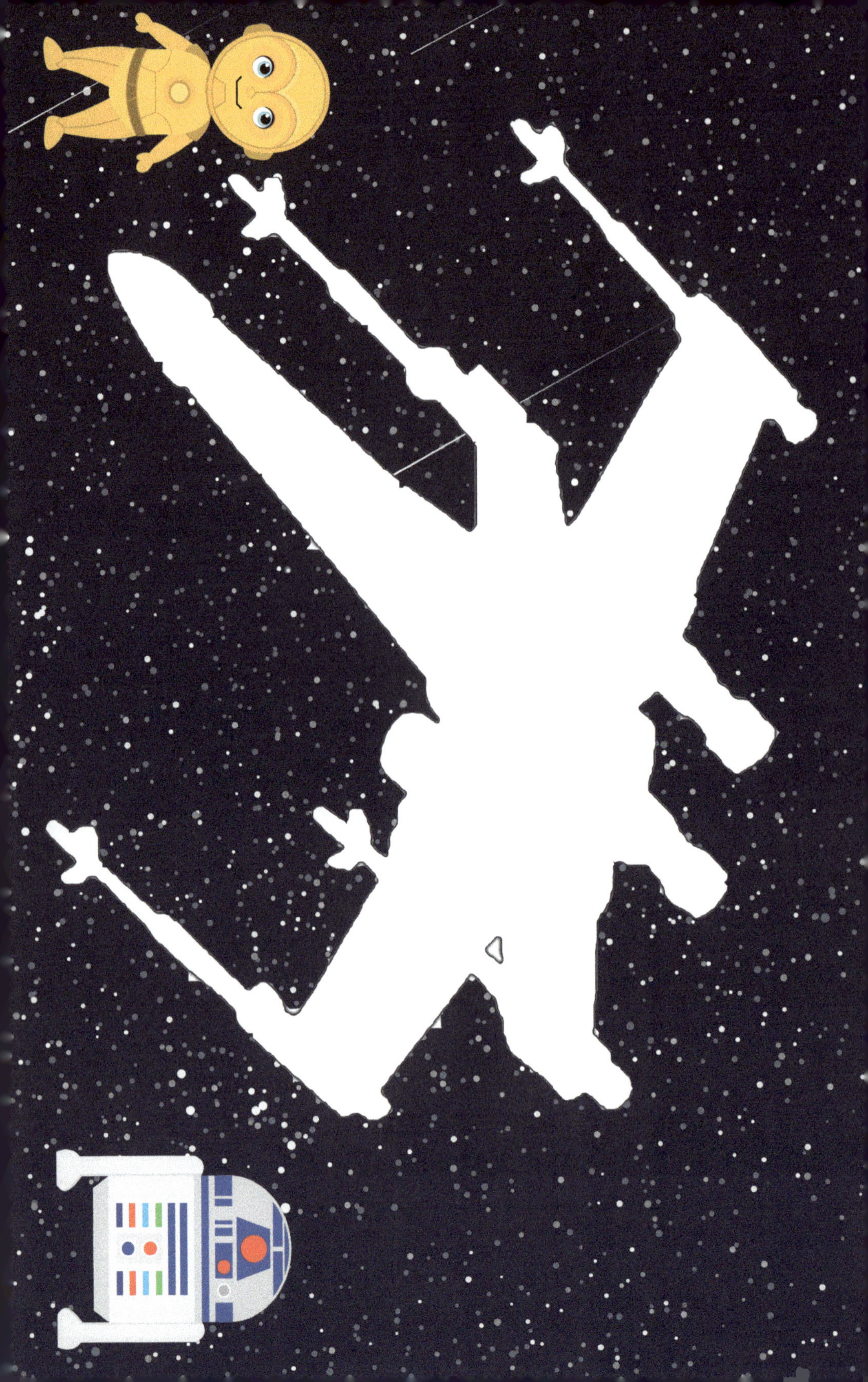

Star Star Star Star Star Star Star Star Star Star
Wars Wars Wars Wars Wars Wars Wars Wars Wars Wars

Frozen Fun

Draw a line from each character to their scrambled up names

NSVE

SFOTRFIK

NAAN

SNHA

SLAE
ALFO

Look What I Got!

Souvenir Coin Page
Glue your stamped coins here, if you'd like!

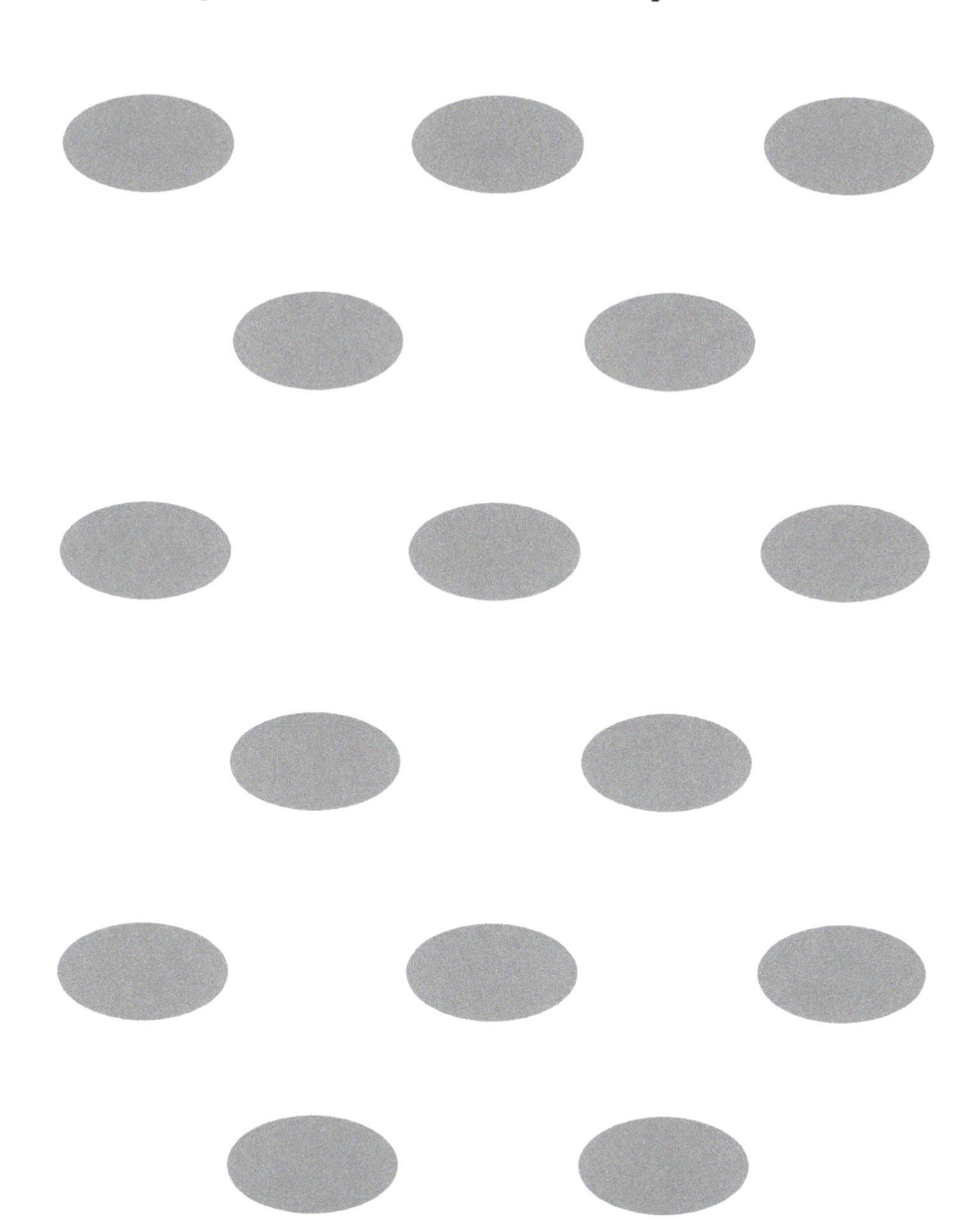

Recap

My favorite ride to go on was _____
because it was _____

I loved meeting _____
because _____

My favorite thing I ate was _____

I didn't like _____
because _____

I wish _____
_____

Some funny things that happened were
_____
_____
_____
_____
_____

My Handprint

Have an adult help you leave your handprint with paint, marker, or by tracing!

My Disney Vacation

Draw your favorite memory from your Disney vacation!

Lightning Source UK Ltd.
Milton Keynes UK
UKHW051144110419
340860UK00009B/82/P